I0457264

WHO DID GOD CREATE YOU TO BE?
A Prophetic Spiritual Journal

SHERRIE A. HILL, D. MIN.

LAEL PUBLISHING

WHO DID GOD CREATE YOU TO BE?
A Prophetic Spiritual Journal

by Sherrie A. Hill, D. Min.
Published by The Lael Agency
Winston Salem, North Carolina
www.LaelAgency.com

Paperback ISBN - 978-1-954433-07-6
Hardback ISBN - 978-1-954433-08-3

Author's Photo:
Bobby and Freda Edwards

Author's contact:
Email: MayHill107@aol.com
Website: SherrieAHill.com

First Edition

Printed in the United States of America.

DEDICATION

To God, for who He created me to be when He said to me, I knew you before your parents knew you in your mother's womb, and for whispering in my ear what to say as he speaks through me to others. He taught me a valuable lesson, which was that I am not responsible for people accepting nor rejecting His word: my assignment is to simply allow Him to speak through me, and the person who rejects His word is rejecting Him and not me, so I should never take offense to how a person responds to His word.

To my parents, Bishop Johnny L. Hill, Sr. and Evangelist Helen A. Hill, for being exemplary role models of Christians. I thank them for the spiritual seeds planted within my heart, and for exposing me to the things of God and teaching me to reverence God both as a child and as an adult.

ACKNOWLEDGEMENTS

To my sister, Dr. Gwendolyn A. Hill, the one person who is always there encouraging and supporting me no matter what, for if God says to do or say it, go forward. I love you.

To my brothers Johnny, Stephen, Alex, and their families: I am so proud of them being the men and women of God that they are. I love you.

To my spiritual parents, Bishop J. C. Hash, Sr. and Lady Joyce Hash, for their spiritual covering and continued prayers over me as well as teaching the true word of God and being true examples of Christian leaders of God's people. I love you both.

CONTENTS

INTRODUCTION

Many years ago, my mother dreamed she saw me in the ocean, and we never knew what that dream meant. Years later after she's left to be with the Lord, He spoke to my heart and informed me that my mother saw my baptism in the Holy Spirit preparing me for the life I now live, serving Him and His people with His Rhema word. The photo on the cover of this book represents the type of body of water that I can imagine my mother may have seen in her dream, because she was truly bothered by that dream, and she continued praying for my protection. Just imagine as a mother, seeing your child in a body of water like that photo and not understanding the meaning. I'd think years of fear would be the order of the day if I was a mother. That level of fear would only be defeated by a **Born-Again** mother, the Word of God, fasting, and praying. Needless to say, my mother became a Minister of the Gospel, and she knew that God would protect me, no matter what.

Searched on Google
What does flowing water symbolize?
Symbol of Change: Water is commonly depicted as a symbol of change due to its flow and movement. It's

never constrained to one location, and it changes its form to become a river, waterfall, sea, or ocean.

What does water symbolize spiritually?
With remarkable regularity across human cultures, water has been used to communicate **the sacred value of life; the spiritual dimension of purification, protection, and healing; and the profound meaning of suffering and redemption in human life.**

What does flowing water mean in the Bible?
In the Old Testament, flowing or "living" water stands for ***God's faithful and lasting provision for his people.*** *From the opposite direction, from above, God's presence is announced by powerful, dramatic, life-giving storms.*

Does water symbolize the Holy Spirit?
"Rivers of living water" represent the Holy Spirit's presence and power poured out on Jesus' followers. The Spirit's presence points to his cleansing and sanctifying work in the hearts of God's children.

My spiritual journals are words that the Lord spoke to my heart. I spent time in the closet just listening to what the Lord was saying to me.

Remember, these words were for me personally, so if you read something that makes your inner spirit jump inside of you, then that word is also meant for you.

God is always talking, but are you listening? He will speak to you in a whisper, through another person, or through a billboard, a bumper sticker, a song, a sound, and a dream, just to list a few of my experiences.

I asked the Lord, what should the title of my second book be? The only thing I heard was SARIBA. Many years ago, during a very intense prayer time about what I was experiencing in my life (i.e., running out of money, running out of food, no job, and more) in the midst of praying, the Lord said to me, "your parents named you Sherrie, but I named you Sariba." I cried and wept until it felt like my eyes were swollen. I was in such a state of shock that when I finally got myself together, I called a friend and told her about my experience, my new name Sariba.

I was desperate to find out what Sariba meant, and my friend informed me that she had heard of a blind prophetess who was known to be excellent at interpretation of names. I was introduced to this prophetess only via telephone and from 1996 to this year of 2022, I still have never met her.

The prophetess informed me that the name Sariba means "Woman of Grace and Favor" and so much more that she shared with me about who I am to Him. I am simply honored that God would give me a new name as He did with those in the Bible.

Abram to Abraham – Genesis 17 – A Father of Many Nations
Sarai to Sarah – Genesis 17 – Blessed Her
Jacob to Israel – Genesis 32:22 – Let My People Go
Saul to Paul – Acts 13:9 – The Changed Christian Man
Simon to Peter – John 1:42 – Rock

What does it mean when God gives you a new name?

The name given by God is the name that will lead us to God's promises. Abram's name to Abraham, Sarai's to Sarah, Jacob's to Israel, and Simon's to Peter – through those names God gave new beginnings, new hopes, and new blessings. A name is a prayer.

What is the significance of a new name?

When several people in the Old and New Testament had a spiritual awakening by coming to God on a new or deeper level, He gave them a new name, **a new identity that redefined their lives.** No longer would they be defined by their old ways, but rather, be called and realized by their new names.

My question to you is, has God given you a new name and you simply ignored Him? Start listening closer to what He is saying to you. Shut down the loud noise and spend time listening to what He is saying. He might be giving you a new name that will lead you to His promises for you. Don't miss your promises from God. He has so much to say and give to you, if you simply spend the time in fellowship with Him.

I pray that you will receive what God has in store for you as you read my personal spiritual journals inspired by God. I only share them because God said to do so, otherwise they would remain personal.

May God bless you in your spiritual journey with Him.

Chapter 1

PROPHETIC SPIRITUAL JOURNALS

Rhema Words from the Lord

July 23, 2013 (9:15 a.m.)

Purposefully give time to God each morning. You saw and admired how those of the Islamic faith spend time with their God every day, men, women, and children, but they do not claim me as their God, yet they do more than those that claim me as their God.

Always busy, not spending planned time to hear what I have to say daily. Start with 30 mins, then one hour each day in the morning after dropping father at daycare. You saw unity in the movie, you saw knowledge and strength also, but I want to give you wisdom to solve any problem or need you may have. The only way is spending quiet time with me daily. Planned time with me; honoring me; giving thanks to me; respecting me; trusting me. Give me you each day and you will always have answers to your questions.

Be still and be quiet as I speak to your spirit.

Yield your spirit, mind, and body to me daily. Read a verse to keep your spirit man fed daily. Repent each time you say something negative because it cancels out the good when you speak negatively. Just as you tell your friend Stan to stop his cursing words, negative words have the same end results, destroys the good.

You both have greatness in you, but the only way for that greatness to be released from you is that you receive wisdom. You are in this world, but you are not of this world. You cannot function like everyone else, for you are Spirit Beings, you function in the Spirit to produce the Natural of this world. Few have tapped into the realm where I will take you, but you must follow my instructions.

Many have tapped into the dark side to glorify themselves and they will be destroyed because what they received came from Me, they have used it to glorify themselves and Satan. They will begin to drop like flies because they did not repent and use their gift I gave them to glorify Me. It is time for those who really have Me in their hearts and will use their spiritual gifts to glorify Me. Greatness will come, but this next group will stay humble and give all the honor back to Me from whence their gifts came.

You have both been chosen to be among this next group that I have touched and anointed to use My unique gifts that man will never understand. The only way to grow in these gifts is to spend that purposeful, quiet time with me as I instruct you. This is a new season, and you are both a part of this new season. A season of change, signs, wonders, miracles, and healings. Keep yourselves clean inside and out in order to perform the gifts I have chosen for you.

Spending quiet time with Me must be your new lifestyle in order for the gifts to flow through you. Nothing good on this earth will be withheld from you because of who you are in Me and I in you.

July 29, 2013 (10:00 a.m.)

Read the King James version of the Bible. Other Bibles are good but they are words that man interpreted. I gave the inspired Words to Matthew, Mark, Luke, and John. The words I gave them are Spirit, Anointed. Man has diluted or polluted My Words already given in the King James version of the Bible. When you read these Words, I am speaking to you. The words of the other bibles are not my Words, but what man has created from their own interpretation of My inspired Words that I gave Matthew, Mark, Luke, and John.

To receive My Spirit, read My Words that are filled with My Spirit, not man's spirit of what they think I was saying. As you read My Words, the Holy Spirit will reveal My pure Words to you. Smith Wigglesworth and Kathryn Kuhlman read My Spirit-filled Words and their anointing was powerful because they did not spend hours reading a diluted or polluted version of My word, but the Spirit Filled and not opinions of man.

July 30, 2013 (10:30 a.m.)

Be careful what you say, for as you can see, you can receive what you say (i.e. Salt movie, boxes at Walmart within mins. of asking). When you speak, things are created in the atmosphere when you utter those words. Whether negative or positive, they are created. Be more conscience/ aware of what you say. Just as I hear your words, Satan also hears your words.

Create only good with your words you speak. The tongue is power, it can destroy or build. Make sure you are building up and not destroying with your tongue.

August 1, 2013 (9:17 a.m.)

Stay in peace. The enemy will try to pull you out, but keep your heart and mind on things that are good and excellent, things that are eternal, not things that are temporary. Call My son Jesus' name to get back into the realm of peace and positive thinking and the enemy will flee immediately.

Lean not unto your own understanding, but in all your ways, acknowledge Me and I will direct your path. Nothing is impossible for Me, but you must continue believing. My Word is truth and My Word is life. Stand on My Word: no matter what people say or do, you stand.

You will encounter many that are demon-possessed; that's why you are so drawn to them. You must stay prayed up and fasted in order to defeat the enemy and set people free. You are seeing via media what you will be performing, delivering others from Satan himself. It is Real, Satan is Real. He will defeat those who are not prepared.

Get prepared, study My Word, and study those who are generals in fighting demons. You are a demon defeater, but you are not trained. You must get trained in order to defeat the demons you will encounter in the future.

August 5, 2013 (10:25 a.m.)

Learn to enjoy the moments in life. Allowing your thoughts to run too far ahead in time causes stress in your body, which causes sickness in your body. Stress is another trick of Satan to destroy your spirit, mind, and body. Stay in peace by enjoying the moments in life that people take for granted. Take the time to enjoy My creations, take the time to smell My fragrance. Slow down, stop being always in a hurry, for you will miss what I am saying and what I am doing. Enjoy life, don't just endure life.

Staying in peace keeps your body healthy, internally and externally. The most beautiful sound is peace and quietness. Learn to tune out the sounds of the world and enter My world of peace and quietness, in the court of the Holy of Holy. That is where you will find Me. Not in the noises of the world.

August 6, 2013 (11:58 a.m.)

Be still and relax. Do not internalize the problems of others. Keep it external so that their problems do not penetrate your spirit. Shake it off and get back into a peaceful mode.

Transferring of spirits is Real. That's why you have to be careful of the people you are around. You take on the spirit of others if you do not know how to guard your spirit.

August 7, 2013 (9:20 a.m.)

Remember to always search the scripture for the word on

the subject you have a need or wants. Pray My Words, believe My Word, and you will therefore receive what you prayed for because it is in My Word.

My Word will never return void. The angels will be busy accomplishing it because My Word is true, it has to come forth. The only way My Word ceases and the angels stop is that you stop believing and do something out of My Will. If you do, quickly repent and what you have prayed for will come forth. It will come from the spirit realm to the natural realm. You shall have what is in My Word. Faint not; keep believing until it is manifested. If you feel yourself wavering, say "I still believe no matter what it looks like or feel like, I Believe." This is the secret to having what you want or need.

Allow no person, place, or thing persuade you differently than what you believe. That's why you cannot always say what's in your heart of hearts of what you want or need and that you are believing for it, because Satan is always, always listening, and he is always, always plotting to stop the Word that you are believing. He will use people, places, and things to stop the Word you are believing.

Rejoice in your heart until the manifestation has arrived. Remember, Satan will tell you that it will not happen; you tell him that it is written, and quote the Word back to him and he will flee.

Remember, My Word will create My Will. In order for that to happen, your will must be My Will and nothing can stop it.

August 8, 2013 (10:47 a.m.)

I woke up this morning with the name Harry on my tongue. I asked my sister if she knew anyone in our family by the name of Harry.

She did not, but I remembered I'd seen a video with the title Harry Flowers with waterfalls and such glorious beauty. My sister suggested, during my 30 minute prayer time, to play the video and see what the Lord will say while watching the video. Below is the result.

Artist – William Orbit

Album – Strange Cargo 3

Track Title – Harry Flowers

See My creations; I control the ocean, the birds, the

mountains, the hills. See the beauty of My creations, man cannot control. The fish move at My command, the waters move at My command.

I control the clouds, the direction in which they flow: whether they be white or dark, I control. See My touch in all My creations. See the sun, the moon: I determine which will rise. I am that I am, Man has no control.

My creations are submissive to Me. Man has a choice to be submissive or not. Those that are submissive are blessed; those that are not are cursed.

Like the eagle, learn when to soar and when to just be still. My creations represent Me. Everything I created has a purpose.

My beauty can be enjoyed or a tragedy, depending on how man uses My beauty. The waterfall is beautiful, but only if man use wisdom; My mountains are beautiful, but only if man uses them wisely. My oceans are beautiful, but only if man uses them wisely; my sun is beautiful, but only if man uses it wisely.

Just to watch the beauty of My creations is a heavenly experience until man makes the wrong choice and they become a tragedy.

- Man can choose Me or Death
- Life can be Easy or Hard
- My creations are serene. I am that I am, you choose.
- You choose Day or Night in your life.
- I am the Day, Satan is the Night

August 9, 2013 (12:05 noon)

You are the light of the world. Let your light defeat the darkness of the world by the way you speak, dress, walk, and act. You represent Me in this world. I am meek and mild, but I am also bold. Be bold as a lion when you encounter the devil. You cannot be passive. The devil preys on passivity. He's afraid of boldness because he knows he does not have a chance to defeat a bold spirit.

Be kind, but do not be used or taken advantage of. Be discerning of who you can help and of who is trying to manipulate. Manipulation is witchcraft; have no tolerance for it. In the end it will destroy. Do not let the dark put out the light.

This country will come to its knees because of the spirit of manipulation. Many will be lost, but My children will be saved from the disaster that will come. Because I am not first in this country, Satan is their God and the end will mean destruction.

Stay close to the altar, for the destruction will surely come. This country was free when they trusted Me, but when they turned their back on me, they fell into bondage. This country is in a timeline of destruction. Too much acceptance of sin, because of money, power, and fame. Sin is sin, there is no compromising. There is no fear of Me and no reverence towards Me, and for this purpose, the end will be destruction. When I remove My arms of protection, Satan will have his way.

Stay close to the altar.

August 12, 2013 (10:05 a.m.)

Enjoy the peace and quiet; I will keep you in perfect peace whose mind is stayed upon Me. Yield all to Me, and stay in peace.

I will restore all if you simply yield it all to Me. I will Bless you with more, if you yield all to Me.

August 13, 2013 (9:15 a.m.)

Speak with authority to My creations and they shall come forth. The angels wait for your commands. Too many times My children do not speak with authority and boldness, and they never receive what they ask for. Timidness and passivity will not get the results you want. Be aggressive, bold, and courageous when you speak. Remember it is My spirit speaking through you, and I have all power and authority. You can enjoy Heaven on Earth. I have given you dominion. The unsaved have learned My principles; it is time for the saved to learn and use My principles. My people are blessed, not poor; healed, not sick. Use the power that is within you. Tap into the Source, for I am that Source. Bless Me, honor Me, and glorify My Name, and you will tap into Me.

This is the secret of those that practice witchcraft: they honor their source who is Satan and they tap into the darkness, but their end will be destruction for There Shall Be No Other God Before Me. Their end will be death in the pool of fire and not eternal life with Me.

Remember, to those who much is given, much is required. The unsaved give their souls to Satan; You must give your Spirit, Mind, and Body to Me.

Repeat 100x daily, the following words to saturate your Spirit Man.

Father in the Name of Jesus, I Bless you; Honor you and I Glorify your Name, in the Name of Jesus.

1. Father in the name of Jesus, I Bless you, Honor you and I Glorify your Name, in the name of Jesus
2. Father in the name of Jesus, I Bless you, Honor you and I Glorify your Name, in the name of Jesus
3. Father in the name of Jesus, I Bless you, Honor you and I Glorify your Name, in the name of Jesus
4. Father in the name of Jesus, I Bless you, Honor you and I Glorify your Name, in the name of Jesus
5. Father in the name of Jesus, I Bless you, Honor you and I Glorify your Name, in the name of Jesus
6. Father in the name of Jesus, I Bless you, Honor you and I Glorify your Name, in the name of Jesus
7. Father in the name of Jesus, I Bless you, Honor you and I Glorify your Name, in the name of Jesus
8. Father in the name of Jesus, I Bless you, Honor you and I Glorify your Name, in the name of Jesus
9. Father in the name of Jesus, I Bless you, Honor you and I Glorify your Name, in the name of Jesus
10. Father in the name of Jesus, I Bless you, Honor you and I Glorify your Name, in the name of Jesus
11. Father in the name of Jesus, I Bless you, Honor

you and I Glorify your Name, in the name of Jesus

12. Father in the name of Jesus, I Bless you, Honor you and I Glorify your Name, in the name of Jesus

13. Father in the name of Jesus, I Bless you, Honor you and I Glorify your Name, in the name of Jesus

14. Father in the name of Jesus, I Bless you, Honor you and I Glorify your Name, in the name of Jesus

15. Father in the name of Jesus, I Bless you, Honor you and I Glorify your Name, in the name of Jesus

16. Father in the name of Jesus, I Bless you, Honor you and I Glorify your Name, in the name of Jesus

17. Father in the name of Jesus, I Bless you, Honor you and I Glorify your Name, in the name of Jesus

18. Father in the name of Jesus, I Bless you, Honor you and I Glorify your Name, in the name of Jesus

19. Father in the name of Jesus, I Bless you, Honor you and I Glorify your Name, in the name of Jesus

20. Father in the name of Jesus, I Bless you, Honor you and I Glorify your Name, in the name of Jesus

21. Father in the name of Jesus, I Bless you, Honor you and I Glorify your Name, in the name of Jesus

22. Father in the name of Jesus, I Bless you, Honor you and I Glorify your Name, in the name of Jesus

23. Father in the name of Jesus, I Bless you, Honor you and I Glorify your Name, in the name of Jesus

24. Father in the name of Jesus, I Bless you, Honor you and I Glorify your Name, in the name of Jesus

25. Father in the name of Jesus, I Bless you, Honor you and I Glorify your Name, in the name of Jesus

August 15, 2013 (11:20 a.m.)

Nothing is too good to be true for My children. I am in the Blessing business. All My children have to do is ask, believe, and receive; when it is My will, it shall be. All good things are in My will. Do not hesitate to receive what I have already blessed you with. Take it, it's yours.

Move forward when I say move forward. Blessings come your way daily; many pass by because you do not always see in the spirit that it's your blessing. Grab hold of your blessings. Do not allow Satan to stick his ugly head up and steal your blessings. What's yours is yours from Me, but as I did with the Israelites, Move when the Clouds Move, not after they've already Moved.

You are in the Season of Blessings. Grab them, let none of them pass you by. Capture them and hold on to them; do not let them escape or get past you for the next person in line to receive them. This is your season. Seize the moment!

There is a door of opportunity open Now! Do not let that door close before you grab your blessings.

August 16, 2013 (9:50 a.m.)

Be still and let My anointing saturate you from the inside out, from the crown of your head to the soles of your feet.

Pray- Saturate me Father with your anointing in the name of Jesus.

August 19, 2013 (9:05 a.m.)

Those that worship Me must worship Me in spirit and in truth, for I am Holy, I am Spirit, I am not Human. Do not pray to me as though I am a mere man. Reverence Me for who I am. I am God, the God of Almighty; all Power; all Authority. I am in all Places; I am eternal and not temporary, as the things of this world are.

I knew you before the beginning of time. I created you to be like Me: a spirit, not a mere mortal of this world. I gave you power over the enemy, authority over the enemy. Use

what I have given to you to stop the enemy that has come against My people.

Stay in the spirit realm in order to fight demons; you will win if you stay in the spirit and not in the natural realm.

You look at your body; that is not who you are. Your Spirit is who you are. Continue feeding your Spirit with My Word, fasting, and praying.

You have spiritual eyes to see, ears to hear, and a tongue to speak; use them for My Glory.

August 20, 2013 (10:15 a.m.)

Consistently doing what I tell you to do is the secret to your success. Not being persuaded by others is the secret to your success. Not being like others is the secret to your success. Not doubting My Word is the key to your success, the key to unlock every door in your life. Everything is at your fingertips; because of My favor upon you, doors are open right now. Do not let them shut. You clear the way for others once shut for them. You are the bridge to the other side for others to walk across and enter into their destiny. Your obedience to Me determines their destiny, so hear My Word and do My Word, because what you hear and do will determine someone else's destiny.

Prosperity begets Prosperity, Poverty begets Poverty, Death begets Death.

Do My Word or Not Do My Word, begets Judgment.

August 21, 2013 (9:50 a.m.)

Receive My power to heal the sick, raise the dead, and heal the broken-hearted. Believe My power flows through you; accept My power flowing through you. As My son Jesus does, Say what I say, and Do what I do, when I say do.

Always remember My touch on your forehead on August 20, 2013 in the wee hours of the night. Continue walking where I walked, taught, healed, delivered, and set free. As I watch you, your mother is also watching. Her presence is with you. The body is dead, but her Spirit lives on.

As you continue to tell her that you love her, she hears your spirit, because she is All Spirit. She is yet alive with Me.

August 22, 2013 (9:00 a.m.)

Repenting of sins is the only way to return to Me. When you sin, blessings are put on hold until True Repentance takes place.

Let not the sun go down before you repent because you carry the sin to the next in your life. Any amount of time that passes without repentance is dangerous for you because it will give Satan the open door to you and destroys you until you return to Me. Quick Repentance is necessary; without it, you give Satan the opportunity to steal, kill, and destroy. His ways never change towards My people.

Sin is any person, place, or thing you put before Me. Sin is Lust of the Eye, Lust of the Flesh, and the Pride of life, and I will forgive, but True Repentance is required.

Remember, I look at the Heart and man looks at the Outside.

August 23, 2013 (11:00 a.m.)

Never feel oblivious or nonchalant about doing good. I

see every seed you plant. You will get the reward for the seeds you planted. Sew good seeds, reap good seeds; sew bad seeds, reap bad seeds. It's Harvest Time for you. The seeds you planted are now returning to you a hundred-fold. Such that you will not have room to receive them all, and you will be filled to overflowing.

Rejoice! It's Harvest Time!

Get Ready to receive your Harvest!!!

Examples of Harvest Time recently received:

$500.00 – unexpected in personal account
$5000+ – school
$5000+ – school
$5000+ – house closing
$50.00 – BK (friend)

August 26, 2013 (11:30 a.m.)

Rejoice! Again I say, Rejoice, for the things I am going to do in your life. Your season has come for the manifestation of your Blessings.

Rejoice, again I say Rejoice. Many will be envious and

jealous, some of them within your family, but they will need more of Me to receive the Blessings they desire for themselves. When they ask you what did you do? Direct them to Me and I will tell them that I am their Source for everything and they will need to tap into their source; that is Me, Not Man. Man will never Bless the way I Bless. Man's Blessings are temporal, My Blessings are Eternal.

Rejoice and Rest in My Word.

It's Settled.

August 27, 2013 (11:50 a.m.)

I am your Strength at all times.

I am your Guide at all times.

I am your Peace at all times.

I am your Joy at all times.

I am your Comforter at all times.
I am that I am, Everything to you and for you. Release Me to be all for you, and I will be in every situation or circumstance in your life.

Keep your inner ears and spiritual eyes open so that you can hear when I speak and see where I should tell you to do.

I will tell you when, were, why, how, and who. I will direct your path, if you submit all to Me. I will not force Myself on you.

Your life will be full of joy, peace, and happiness if you simply give control to Me. I am Everything for you; there is no other.

August 28, 2013 (9:20 a.m.)

Remember, do not take offenses. It's the Devil's method of stopping your Blessings. Repent quickly and get back in peace. Remember, some people around you are assigned to offend because Satan is their Father. They do not understand; they are cursing themselves every time they fulfill their assignment.

Take no thought on what the offender says or does, for they are only cursing and placing themselves closer to the Lake of Fire at the end of their life, and they do not know that. Some know, but do not believe their end result, but it will still be the Lake of Fire if they do not repent and give their lives to Me.

Do not respond to them, but stay in Peace and remember, their end is the Lake of Fire. Their words cannot hurt you, but will destroy them.

Remember, offenses stop your Blessings and curses the offender.

Pray this prayer: I receive no offenses and I give no offenses. I stay in God's Peace.

August 29, 2013 (9:50 a.m.)

Be still and know that I am God. I will do what I said. I cannot lie; when I say it, it is so. Just believe and trust Me. Stay in the Spirit of Faith in Me and My Word for all things.

I will not always tell you how it will happen; just believe and have faith that it will.

Pray the following prayer: Father in the name of Jesus, I trust You and I trust Your Word.

August 30, 2013 (11:10 a.m.)

Sing A New Song Unto Me, for it makes me smile to see you worshipping Me. It convicts the hearts of sinners, it sets the captives free, it heals the broken-hearted, it encourages the discouraged. It changes the atmosphere from Dark to Light, from sorrow to happiness, from defeated to victory. Sing, I say, a new song unto Me.

Those that are lost will be won; those that are despised will be embraced. Those that are lonely will be comforted; those that are sad will be joyful.

Sing A New Song Unto Me.

September 6, 2013 (10:15a.m.)

Breathe in and breathe out and know that I gave you life, not man. I am the Author and the Finisher of your life, not man. Too many people continue to depend on man for their lives. I am the only one who can give life eternally and take life eternally.

Do not put man on a pedestal because chances are, he will disappoint you when you least expect it, which will bring about a sense of devastation in your life when you put man first. Man is human and is subject to me.

Keep Me first in everything and stay focused on Me and not man.

Hear My voice and I will lead you into all things that are good, acceptable, and My perfect will.

September 9, 2013 (11:00a.m.)

The more time you spend with Me, the more you will see in the spirit realm: people, places and things that you will not be able to explain, other than I allowed you to see in My realm.

The more time you spend with Me, the more you will be able to audibly hear My voice, not just small whispers as you have already heard.

Do not be afraid of what you see nor of what you hear; this is My way of letting you know that you have tapped into the Spirit realm. Nothing can hurt you, so embrace your new experience. This experience is only unusual or strange for those people that have never had the experience. There is a cost you have to pay for this experience. The price is spending time with Me, studying My Word, fasting, praying, and yielding your spirit, mind and body to me.

The experiences increase as you mature in Me. You have had such experiences, but not at the level that comes with maturity in Me.

You will be able to lay your hands on the sick and they shall recover because I will Flow through you. I will simply use your vessel. I will tell you where to touch and who is ready to receive My touch. There are many people not healed because they will not believe what My son has already done on the cross for them. Their hearts are in conflict with their minds and their minds (the reasoning area) keeps them in bondage of disbelief, and therefore, they will not and cannot receive Me.

The touching is simply a point of contact and agreeing with what My Son has already done on the cross. Doctors play a part in some healing processes because I have told them where the problems are and through their training, they have the knowledge. My people perish for lack of knowledge. Some doctors acknowledge that it was Me, and some do not. Those that do not, will have to give an account to Me for taking My Glory. Those that do acknowledge that it was Me, will continue to be blessed and will have eternal life.

Whatever gifts I freely give, never take My glory to be your glory.

Pray the following: Thank you Father in the name of Jesus for your Spirit Flowing out of Me into others for healing, deliverance, and setting the captives free in the name of Jesus. I will not take Your Glory as My Glory. Thank You for the mantle of Your power, in the name of Jesus.

September 10, 2013 (8:35a.m.)

Hold tight to your Faith. Never let it go. Satan attempts to make things look like the opposite of what your Faith says, but do not fall for his game. He is a liar, and the truth is not in him. Just like I cannot lie, he can only lie.

Never believe what he says or does; it will always be the opposite of My Word to you. Continue to make the choice to have Faith and believe My Word. No matter the circumstances, it will always work for your good.

Pray: Thank You for Your divine favor and Your divine power. I walk in the office of Faith as Abraham did.

September 17, 2013 (9:53a.m.)

You are Free when you are in My presence; Satan cannot enter in. Practice being in My presence and enjoy the peacefulness that I have for you. Even in the environment of others, you can still be in My presence by staying focused on Me and not the cares of this world. Take no thought for tomorrow, for tomorrow will take care of itself.

Stay in My presence by whispering My Son's name, Jesus. You will feel immediate peace and calmness when you whisper His name. His name is a strong tower for you to run to when everything around you feels like it is falling apart. That's the enemy making every attempt to draw you away from Me.

Stay in peace and enjoy My presence, and nothing and no one can touch you. No problem can touch your heart if you practice staying in My presence.

Leaders must stay in My presence to hear Me clearly and do what I have called them to do. Leaders must be so close to Me to know when it is My voice and when it is the voice of Satan attempting to trick them.

Leaders must stay in My presence so that they are not shaken when the cares of life are upside down.

Leaders must let Me do the leading and they must follow My every command and not allow man to lead them. I am the Master Leader, there is none other.

Allow Me to lead you and all will work for your good.

September 19, 2013 (9:53a.m.)

Die to self and live an eternal life. Remember; put no person, place, or thing before Me. Keep the purposeful prayer time with me in order to hear my words to you. I will tell you how to solve problems that may arise. Do not put business before spending time with Me. Do not get so busy that you slack on spending time with Me. Now that your season has changed to abundance, do not forget Me. Keep your prayer time with Me; keep your prayer time with Me.

You will get the answers to your questions when you have spent time with Me.

Remember, I am a jealous God; spending time with Me is not an option for you, it is a COMMAND.

Stop! And hear Me first. Remember how the Muslins STOPPED and spent time with their god. It is a Command for you to STOP and spend time with your God and you can have Eternal life. The Muslins do not have a god that can give them eternal life and yet, they are Compelled to STOP EVERYTHING at a certain time and give Honor and Praise to their God. They believe in their god. You must show that you believe in me, by your Action towards Me. You can enjoy Heaven on Earth and Eternal Life.

Give me the Honor and Praises that I long for. It is REQUIRED to be the Leaders I have ordained you to be in this sinful world.

September 20, 2013 (10:20 a.m.)

Leaders are strong, yet meek and humble
Delegate not Dictate
Commanding not Demanding

Soft and Courageous
Discerning not Blind
A Hearer and a Doer
Decision Makers not Passive
Aggressive, Assertive
Determined, Defeaters
Humbled but not Pushovers
Walk Through, not Stop in Park or Neutral
Firm but Kind
Repent and do not Offend
Passionate, Strong Willed
Listeners, Fully Persuaded
Independent and Dependent
Yielded Spirits, Mind. and Body
Competent & Confident
Peaceful, Progressive not Digressive
Servants & Leaders
Bold as a Lion, Soft as a Kitten
Givers not Takers
Set Apart from the Pack
Completely Yielded to Me

September 23, 2013 (10:50 a.m.)

Satan is a creature of habits, he has no new tricks. His tricks will always be Lust of the Eye, Lust of the Flesh, and the Pride of Life. Stay focused and alert to his tricks.

Keep a watchful eye, a spiritual ear, and a clean tongue. Keep your thoughts clean and positive. Remember, he plants things in the mind for you to speak out. Be careful what you say about yourself as well as others. He does not want you to have what I have for you and he will do everything to slow it down and try to stop it. But know that he was defeated when My Son went to the cross, took the Keys from Satan in Hell, and rose with Me.

Satan will only have the power that you give to him. Satan will only have the authority that you give to him. Remember his tricks, and they can come from any direction.

Stay focused, alert, watchful; spiritual eyes, spiritual ears, clean tongue, and an open heart. Quickly repent when you catch yourself out of line.

September 24, 2013 (10:15a.m.)

Never allow the devil to make you second-guess what I have already said to you. Repent quickly! Be anxious for nothing. Stay focused, stay in peace, and keep my words in your heart, in your eyes, and on your tongue.

Faith means to step out there even when it does not feel like it is going to happen. Stay out there in Faith anyway!

Repeat: I have what I say I have; I have what I believe I have in my heart.

Once it is settled in your heart, nothing and no one can take that away. Visualize yourself with your desire in your heart and keep it right there until it manifests itself.

Go to the 4th dimension and stay there for a while until it's settled in your heart.

Remember, questioning yourself comes from the devil; part of his tricks, playing with your thoughts.

Tell him to flee your thoughts and he will.

September 25, 2013 (9:00a.m.)

My Word is real, My Word is pure. Drink My Word, it is a daily cure. Medicine for the body, peace for the soul, joy everlasting for those who hold My Word within their hearts. Eat and drink My Word; I Am My Word. Do this in remembrance of Me. My Word will move many mountains, defeat all enemies. Learn how to use My Word, and let it penetrate your every being; and then shall you become like Me, Spirit Being. Keep filling up on My Word daily.

You will become more spirit than flesh being. When you stay in My Word, My Word changes you, not people, place or things.

Commune with Me, with My Word, and through your heavenly language. Those that worship Me, must worship Me in spirit and in truth.

You are in this world, but you are not of this world and therefore you cannot function as the world functions. You are Spirit; tap into the Spirit realm to function in this world and conquer the enemy.

September 26, 2013 (9:00 a.m.)

Do not allow the chains of life to hang around your neck. Break every chain that tries to bind you and Be Free. Say no when you feel a no in your heart; say yes when you feel a yes in your heart. Never compromise with the enemy. Once you start to compromise, he will continue to entangle you until it will be difficult to break loose.

Do not compromise; nothing is worth it.

September 30, 2013 (11:52 a.m.)

Take the time to simply be still and be quiet and listen to the beautiful sound of nothing. This is when you can simply enjoy My peace, peace beyond your understanding.

Your heart beats slowly; every nerve, muscle, gland, and tissue in your body is in a peaceful state. Enjoy the peacefulness; do not allow people, places or things disturb your peace.

See yourself sitting on the white sand at the beach with only the harmonious roaring sound of the water. No people around, no noise of honking horns, no loud voices, no children crying. Just you and the beautiful sound of the ocean.

Enjoy being peaceful.

October 1, 2013 (10:15 a.m.)

Don't worry about your father, for he is in My care. When he cries, he's feeling My presence. He's not grieving, but feeling My presence. He is My child and I will take care of him. He is a Leader in his heart, even though many tried to keep him down. He is a true leader, one who cares more for others than himself.

He will do more for others quicker than the average man because he is a Pastor/Leader at the core of his heart. Continue to honor My leader and you will be blessed. You see a true leader, one that has given Me his entire life, the leader I ordained him to be before he was born. Admire and respect the leader that has been in your entire life; there aren't many left like him.

I have My arms around him. Continue to rejoice and worship Me.

October 2, 2013 (10:00 a.m.)

Make every day a good day because I created every day. Enjoy my creation; whether it be sunshine, rain, snow, or sleet, it's a good day because you are alive to see that day. Always look for the beauty, not the negative.

Negativism brings criticism, which is a spirit that is not of me. Learn to think about what you are going to say before you say the wrong thing. Remember, Satan want you to say the wrong words to stop you from going to the next level in Me for your life. Be very careful with your tongue. There is power and death in the tongue. You have the choice on how to use your tongue. Think before you speak and hear

Me speaking to you.

Slow down and think; as a leader, your destiny depends on what you say and what you think. People that you lead will hang on to your every word, and therefore, you must always remember to think before you speak. Sometimes it will be better not to say anything at all, depending on the situation. You might have an opinion, but it might be better not to offer your opinion at that particular time.

Remember, you be the hearer and I'll speak through you. I will tell you what to say and how.

October 7, 2013 (11:30 a.m.)

Simply trust and believe, do not yield to doubt. My Word is real and true. Keep the Faith; testing comes to try your Faith and to take you to the next level of faith in Me.

My chosen Leaders will go through the Fire, Hills, Mountains, and Valleys, but they will come out of each as Pure Gold, fighting the good fight, spirit to spirit. It's not a physical fight, but a spiritual fight. Stay in the spirit realm. Satan will try to draw you into the physical realm. You will always win in the spiritual realm.

October 8, 2013 (10:56 a.m.)

Practice PRAISING ME at home; DANCING before ME. Spend time shouting and rejoicing before Me; anything that attempts to attach itself to you will have to FLEE!

You cannot rejoice and be depressed at the same time. The JOY of the Lord is your STRENGTH! Too many Christians do not remember that when they are going through trials, testing, and tribulation. Simply DANCE like David danced, and know within your heart, that all is well. All is well because as you REJOICE; you are saying to Me by your action that you give it all to Me. JOY, My JOY is your strength. Keep rejoicing until you feel My strength come upon you. Say, Thank You Jesus while you are rejoicing because whatever you need, in My Will, IT IS DONE!

Rejoicing changes you and your atmosphere, and makes the Devil FLEE! REJOICE! AGAIN, I SAY, REJOICE!

Do not wait until you get to the church house on Wednesday or Sunday services; rejoice right there in your home, right where you are. MY JOY IS INDEED YOUR STRENGTH! Rejoicing is just as important as fasting, praying, trusting, and Believing. Rejoicing takes you out of yourself and focuses on Me, not what's around you and not on people, places, or things when you are really rejoicing before Me.

Rejoicing releases the HEART.

Rejoice because My Word says rejoice!

October 9, 2013 (10:28 a.m.)

Always remember, My Spirit dwells within you.

Many Christians do not really understand that because they have not been taught when they have given their lives to Me. This is why they think it is okay to say or do whatever they like, but they need to know that it is not okay. They grieve My Spirit when they sin and do not repent. They need to understand the word repent. Repent means to turn from their sinful ways and not go back to sin once they have repented; not say they repent in their mind, but it must be in their hearts which is where the change will take place and when they have been set free from their sin.

They must know that they will not be perfect until I return, but they must continue striving for perfection of maturity in Me until I return.

They must understand that I see and hear everything. That I am really omnipotent, omniscient, and omnipresent.

They must understand that Judgment Day will truly come, and it will be at this time that they will either be Mine or Satan's. The way they have lived their lives will determine whom they belong to in the end.

The time is drawing nigh; now they still have a choice, but on the Day of Judgment, they will not have a choice.

October 14, 2013 (10:30 a.m.)

Embrace every day, for every day is a good day that I have made. Do not focus on tomorrow, for tomorrow will take care of itself. Do not ruin today by wondering about tomorrow. Enjoy each day, each moment, each hour, each second.

Stay in peace.

October 15, 2013 (10:36 a.m.)

Stay focused on My Word to you. Do not allow Satan to make you wonder in your mind. Stay focused and tell Satan that you believe what I have said to you. Satan likes playing tricks with your thoughts. You speak to him and tell him to flee from your thoughts. He'll tell you to start doubting My Word because you have not seen the manifestation yet, but do not doubt in your heart. Keep believing and wait for it to come forth. It's already done in the heavenly realm; wait for it to come forth in the earthly realm.

Remember, Faith is the substance of things hoped for the evidence of things not seen. Without faith, it is impossible to please Me. All things are possible for Me to perform, Nothing is impossible for me to do. Man is limited, I am not. Never confuse Me with man. I am God and God alone, and I do not share my Glory with man. Trust Me, not man. Man will fail you; I cannot fail you. All power is in My hands.

October 17, 2013 (11:27 a.m.)

Peace and Tranquility

Peace and Tranquility

Peace and Tranquility comes from Me.

Close your eyes and visualize a waterfall. Hear the sound of the mighty rushing water. You are sitting under the waterfall enjoying My peace and tranquility.

Enjoy the moment. Relax every muscle in your body, relax your mind and stay focused on the sound of the rushing might water, and enjoy My peace and tranquility.

All leaders must take the time out of their busy schedule during the day to enjoy My peace and tranquility. It's a way of getting refreshed and having a renewed spirit, but at the same time energizing yourself for the next task.

Practice having peace and tranquility moments. Just stop everything. Don't say anything during your time of peace and tranquility. Just enjoy the time.

October 22, 2013 (10:30 a.m.)

Distractions exist to keep you from staying focused on Me. You have the power and authority to control your distractions. Say the name of Jesus, with your eyes closed, several times, and you will not be able to be distracted and focus on Jesus at the same time. Distractions will have to flee.

Stay focused on Me; things are not as they appear to be to you. Looking at a cell through a microscope is like blessings are coming your way that you cannot see with the naked eye. I see them coming toward you; you stay focused on Me and know that the blessings are coming.

You have a blessing every day that you cannot see. Practice thanking Me for your blessings for that day and you will not miss what I have in store for you on that particular day. Do not take each day for granted; it's a blessing to see that day as you awaken in the morning. Many will go to sleep at night and not awaken in the morning, but you woke up! Thank Me for that!

October 28, 2013 (12:18 noon)

This is the day that I have made, Rejoice and be glad in it. The enemy will try to make you feel sad and gloomy, but Rejoice. Again, I say Rejoice! All is well.

Remember, stay focused on today, not on tomorrow, for tomorrow will take care of itself. Stay in the spirit realm and meditate on My Word.

October 29, 2013 (10:40 a.m.)

Be anxious for nothing, but be excited about what I'm going to do in your life. Look up and know that I am with you through all things. I am not only with you, but also My Spirit is within you. Consult My Spirit before making any decision and you will never make the wrong decision. I will always tell you to do or say what is best for you. The enemy comes to steal, kill, and destroy, but I come to give life, more and abundantly.

When you truly have peace about making a decision, that's the right decision to make. Anxiety, doubts, and fears are not of Me, but of Satan. Be very aware of how he attempts to lead you into situations that are not of Me.

Seek Me first for your answers to all things.

November. 1, 2013 (11:55 a.m.)

See the many colors of the trees during the autumn season and see My glory. Life is like the many colors of the trees; there is a season for everything. A season to laugh; a season to cry; a season to die to the old ways of doing things and embrace the new in your life.

Your life will go through the many colors. As you see the many colors of the trees, see the many colors of your life – the Good, the Bad, and the Ugly. But I am with you through all of the seasons of your life. The many seasons of your life will help you to mature in Me; draw you closer to Me; to help you understand that life is not always the same as it was yesterday, last year, nor the year before. There will always be seasons in your life; new seasons of your anointing that I have placed within you.

As leaders, as your anointing increases, Satan's targets towards you will also increase. Remember, there is a season of battles and a season of peace. Be prepared for the battles and don't get lost in the peace because Satan is still plotting during your season of peace.

Stay alert, stay focused, and stay faithful during all of your seasons of life.

As you see My glory through the many beautiful colors of the trees, as you mature in Me, many will see My glory in you as My anointing blossom through you.

November 4, 2013 (11:45 a.m.)

Not only as a leader, but also as My chosen one, never allow Satan to stop you from doing what I have told you to do. When you allow him to stop you or make you hesitate, you are allowing him to stop or slow down the destiny of others that I have waiting for the next movement in their lives.

Assignments are made by Me to you to stand in the gap for others. Some you know and some you will not know who they are. You must continue doing and saying what I have called and anointed you to do or say. Remember, if you do not, another person's life is in jeopardy because of what you didn't do or say. I have purpose for what I'm telling you to do or say. It is not for you to always know the purpose nor the outcome or end result.

As a maturing leader, simply obey Me. I work through people in order to make miracles happen for others.

Don't stop the miracles that someone needs that I perform through you. Continue doing, saying, and going as I tell you, not as you think. Your thoughts are not My thoughts.

I have Purpose for everything.

November 7, 2013 (10:30 a.m.)

Leaders are tested and watched not only by Me but by man. Man tests the mind, I test the heart. I know what you will and will not do, but you don't. Life throws many obstacles in your way, but you make the choice to go around, go over, go under, or go through the obstacles that you will encounter.

Pressure forces one to lead or throw in the towel. You will be a great leader only when you allow Me to lead and guide you into and through all things.

As a leader, always listen to Me first to get the answers to any situation and you will stay in peace. Peter was in peace when he walked on the water until he took his eyes off of Me. Never take your eyes off of Me or you will sink in the situation that you will encounter. The enemy is always on the attack because that's who he is.

As leaders, understand who you are and whom you belong to and who Satan is. Understand Satan will use anybody to distract, and any circumstance to distract. When unexpected things happen, laugh and rejoice; you will give Satan a black eye when you laugh instead of getting upset with what you are going through at that moment. Embrace it and go forward; do not get stuck in the situation.

Remember; the closer you get to Me, the more Satan will attack; but know; he will never win because you belong to Me.

November 12, 2013 (9:40 a.m.)

All is well; don't worry about anything because My grace

and favor are upon you. Continue giving to others, planting seeds in the lives of others, and you will continue being blessed beyond what you can ever even imagine.

I am your Father and I will take care of everything concerning you. Continue believing, trusting, and having Faith in Me and My Word.

Rest in Me.

November 14, 2013 (11:05 a.m.)

My anointing destroys every yoke. Nothing can stand under My anointing that dwells within you. Continue feeding My spirit that's within you with My Word, fasting and praying. That's how My anointing gets stronger within you. Keep a clean tongue, clean heart, clean mind, and a clean body.

Remember, you represent me at all times. You were purchased with a price. You belong to Me; you are not your own. I am Alpha and Omega; believe My Word, receive My Word, and trust My Word even more when it comes to your personal life.

November 19, 2013 (6:00 a.m.)

Draw closer to Me as I draw closer to you. You will not be able to see, hear, and do the things I have called you to do unless you draw closer to Me. Do not return to the old way of doing things on a daily basis. Get richer and deeper in Me. As you have already heard through My messengers Evangelists Jeffers and Jessie Duplantis, there is so much more for you to see, hear, and do.

Increasing your relationship with Me is a command, not an option. Obey My command and see My glory. You will touch many lives because I have touched you.

Draw closer to Me and I will draw closer to you.

November 20, 2013 (6:00 a.m.)

Intercede for the church body to catch on fire, that they may see signs, wonders, and miracles. Without My power, it will not happen. Intercede that the church body will allow Me to flow, that they will give Me the time during their services and understand that they must acknowledge My presence and stop church as usual.

Nothing will happen with church-as-usual syndrome.

They should stop being afraid of My power and start using My power so that people can get healed, set free, and delivered.

Playing Church Must Cease.

November 28, 2013 (2:00 p.m.)

Thank You God, for You being God. In charge of everything and everybody. Thank You for Your love, Your power, Your divine favor upon my life and the life of my family. Thank You for no longer allowing my mother to suffer in this world, but to join You in paradise where there is no more weeping and wailing, no more suffering of the things of this world. Thank You for the joy of the Lord being my strength. Thank You for healing me and protecting me and my family.

Thank You for the times we shared with mom and dad at this stage of their lives. Thank you for allowing us to take care of them and not have to place them in nursing homes where they do not know anyone and possibly not be taken care of the way we would want them to be taken care of. Thank You for allowing us to show them the love from our hearts to them and for them being in their right minds to feel the love we have for them.

Father in the name of Jesus, I really do not have adequate words to say thank You and therefore I will simply say that I love You and You are indeed first in my life. Nothing and no one is more important to me than You are. I will continue to do everything You have called me to do. I will continue worshipping You in spirit and in truth. I will continue giving Your word to those who are my assignments.

December 2, 2013 (10:30 a.m.)

There is power in the name of Jesus. The name of Jesus brings light where there is darkness, joy where there is sadness, and understanding where there is ignorance, awareness of righteousness where there is sin. Continue learning how to fight the enemy. Trust the name and power of Jesus and continue seeking My face.

Repeat the following from Prophet T.B. Joshua:

I believe Jesus is my Healer

I believe Jesus is my Solution

My power is greater that Satan's. He has fooled many, but only because they do not know me. They must get to know me, and then they will not have any fear of what Satan tries to do to me.

December 2, 2013 (11:21 a.m.)

Rejoice in everything you go through. Nothing is too hard when you put it in My hands. Celebrate life, remember your mother is with Me rejoicing and enjoying herself. Celebrate her home going on this day that she came to be with Me.

I am Alpha and Omega and the finisher of your Faith. Keep looking up to Me and do not get distracted. That is what Satan wants, for you to be distracted and not spend time with Me, having that intimate time with Me. Learn of Me and more of who you are. Do not allow Satan to steal your time from Me. You make a choice to spend time with Me. Spending time with Me renews your Spirit. You will grow spiritually by spending time with Me.

Chapter 2

PROPHETIC ANOINTING SCRIBE

Prophetic scribes are mandated to release anointed words of the Father, and the target to penetrate is the hearts of men. These words are meant to go the distance. They bring victory to one kingdom while defeating another.

What is a prophetic scribe?

Prophetic scribes are intercessors with revelatory gifts who are also the Holy Spirit's secretaries. They write in a dated journal what the Holy Spirit personally speaks through their Rhema: dreams, visions, trances and anything else that is quickened in all the other many ways there are to hear Him.

The Distinctive Signs of the Prophetic Scribe
By Theresa Harvard Johnson
April 20, 2021
Spiritual Growth

Just as there are distinctive signs and characteristics for spiritual gifts like apostles and prophets, there are also distinctive signs of prophetic scribes.

Those distinctions, when stretched out line-upon-line, unveil layer upon layer of evidence that clearly identifies the release of the scribal anointing operating in the lives of believers today.

There are eight signs easily visible in the lives of those with a scribal calling based on Scripture and biblical scribal history as well as observations and revelation gained through leading, guiding, and mentoring others.

Prophetic Scribal Signs

Individuals with a prophetic scribal anointing:

1. Often pray, intercede. or talk with God through their pen. They tend to work out the issues of their hearts in their notebooks or journals, sharing secret things that only God will hear. In this place, writing has become an ear and a tool used for self-deliverance, healing, impartation, contemplation, joy, building, and adoration to the Father.

2. Write or record from a strong, unplanned, or unrehearsed flow. The words simply stream from the Spirit of the Lord into their hearing and through their recording device or pen. This includes dialogue, novel scenes, songs, poetry, spoken word, the wording of letters, contracts, book content organization, and much more.

3. Can quickly identify God's heart concerning the direction of creative, administrative, or even instructional

literary works. They simply know where key scribal pieces fit and how they should flow. Most often, this is not a learned behavior but a tangible manifestation of the word of knowledge or the word of wisdom.

4. Once awakened by the Lord, experience constant manifestations of their gifting. In other words, they are daily operating in an aspect of their scribal function. This can be likened to the same level of passion one might see in a musician, psalmist, or visual artist. The gifting literally begins to consume and shape their lives.

5. Long and desire to hear the Lord speak to them and through them either creatively, instructionally, or administratively. This includes consistently operating eagerly in creative, instructional, or administrative activities.

6. Have a preoccupation with recording what they see, hear, and/or experience from the Lord. As the gift matures, they begin to experience a desire to share what they receive with others.

7. May have a special gift and anointing to hear and see stories, articles, novels, and books in the lives of or on behalf of others. They walk under a special grace in which they are primarily "recorders" in the kingdom and may or may not write or record extensively for themselves.

8. Experience an urgent call to record everything the Lord releases to them and cannot rest until those things are completed. They often use terms like being compelled or pushed to record or write.

A Prophetic word from God
To Those That Will Hear

April 21, 2022 11:27a.m.

You are not at the end of life yet, you still have time to give your heart to Me. I am waiting for you, I will not pressure you. Remember the things you have gone through and you know in your heart that your only way of escape was through Me.

Time is of the essence for you to yield your heart. Many are dying because of different reasons and many had not given their hearts to Me. Do not let yourself be one of those who are lost for eternity.

My arms were opened wide for them, yet they rejected Me. They chose the things of this world: people, places, and things that were temporary. Even when I saved them from so many times before in their lives, they made the wrong decision and now they will not live in paradise with Me. Satan is their father.

Thus, Saith the Lord.

April 21, 2022 11:36 a.m.

Stay focused upon Me, for I will keep you in perfect peace. Not man's peace but My peace, which is a spirit. Do not focus on the cares of the world, for they will put you in a state of turmoil and that is Satan's plan, to keep you in that state. The spirit of depression, suicide, murder, and stealing is running rampant. You must pray daily to fight against those spirits.

Satan has possessed these people at every level and they no longer have control of themselves because they have given their souls to Satan for lust of the eye, lust of the flesh, and the pride of life. Families are torn apart and they don't understand what's happening to their loved ones, when they used to be so kind and now they simply hate everyone and everything. Fasting, praying, faith, and My written Words are the only solution.

Many churches have compromised, so that anything is acceptable in the house of God, but compromising is not acceptable in my sacred house. I am giving church leaders a small window of time to get their churches in order. The pureness of the Holy Ghost has been lost due to compromising. Church leaders must repent and have their members repent. Things will only get worse if repentance does not take place. The church must look like Me, talk like Me, walk like Me, do as I say, and go where I say go. Stop looking and acting like the world. I will shut many church doors because they are pretending to put Me first, but they are far from Me, I know them not.

Many are going astray because of the pretending in church leaders and members. Many have been in positions too long and there's no room for growth for the spiritual level needed. The leaders of old taught what they knew and many were led by My spirit. In many cases today, that is not happening. Many leaders are being led by the dollar and popularity.

This must stop, saith the Lord. It's time for change in the church. The people are hungry for Me, they need My pure spirit. Release them to be free and see the spiritual and physical growth that will occur. Many musicians and praise teams are performing and not singing to glorify Me, but themselves. It's time for change.

Don't let your church be the next church I shut down, saith the Lord.

June 30, 2022 10:48 a.m. - 11:19a.m.

Place your hand in My hand, you will be safe. Don't look to the left nor to the right. I am up high, keep looking up; Satan wants to distract and destroy. Do not let him open the door to your heart; once he gets a grip of your heart he will move into your soul and your body. Demand him to depart from you and he will. Command him in My name and he will leave. Resist him and he will leave.

Do not be afraid for I am with you; know that I will never leave you. Stay focused on Me and Me alone. Don't look behind; keep going forward to the future, for the past is over. The past will keep you stuck; you will not progress looking back. Smile, have fun, enjoy life. Live and keep going forward. Death tried to claim you several times but I said NO. I have a hedge of protection around you and around your heart. You will not be defeated, for the Destiny I have for you is long life and a successful life.

Believe My Word, live My Word, eat My Word. You will lack for nothing. Everything you need is already done, so just rejoice in My name. I say, rejoice in My name. I will always be with you; I will always be with you. The devil will try to stop you, but he will not be able to. As long as you continue trusting Me, believing in Me, staying focused on Me, surrendering your heart to Me, he cannot touch you. Look up and see Me, hear My voice, I am always with you. My spirit is in you and upon you. You belong to Me; the devil has no authority over you. Believe My Word; go forth in the calling I have placed in you and upon you. Noting and no one can stop you. Yes, go forward in my calling in My Word, in My Way. You will continue to get stronger in Me.

I am in you, I am in you, I am in you. Just yield to Me, completely yield to Me, and I will take you to places and people you never dreamed of, because it's Me and not you, it's Me and not you. Just move forward when I say move forward. Just say what I tell you to say. Remember, it's not you, it's Me, it's Me, you are simply My vessel that I have chosen to speak My mysteries through.

I love you, I love you, you are very special and unusual because I made you that way. People can't understand you because you are not like them. Many are afraid of you because they know that I dwell within you and upon you. Take no thought of them, take no thought of them, just trust me and believe upon Me, take no thought to them. Trust Me and Me alone. I am your protector. No man can protect you the way I protect you. Stay focused on Me and you will see the manifestation of the destiny that I have in store for you. Do not concern yourself with the things of the heart toward man, for man cannot help you with the things I have in store for your destiny. Stay focused on Me.

Continue to listen to certain music that will cause you to write My Word. I speak through certain music that only you can hear My Word through certain sounds. Stay focused, stay focused, and hear what I say to you.

Stay humbled because I will take you to a level in My spirit that you have not experienced before. Don't be afraid, for it is Me; don't be afraid, for it is Me and not Satan speaking to you. Satan has no authority to speak to you. It's Me and Me alone. Don't be afraid; remember you are different, you are unique, you are indeed special. When your mother saw you in water, I did a special anointing of you then; that's what she saw but she didn't understand what she was seeing. I tell you now, I anointed you from the crown of your head to the soles of your feet to write My word, sometimes sing My word when I say sing or when I say write My Word. I anointed you; you will know who to share My Word with because I will always tell you. If it's for the world, it's for the world, or if it's for an individual, I will always tell you.

Remember certain sounds trigger the anointing that I have placed in and upon you. Certain sounds draw that anointing out of you and you can't help yourself because

it's drawing Me to speak through you.
Continue praying in tongues
Speak for Me
Continue using the media to speak My Word
Receive Your Calling
Now Walk In Your Calling

July 5, 2022
PT. 1 - 8:16 a.m.- 8:34 a.m.
PT. 2- 10:00 a.m.

A Word from the Lord

PART 1 8:16 a.m.- 8:34 a.m.

THEY THAT WORSHIP ME MUST WORSHIP ME IN
THE SPIRIT AND IN TRUTH. SURRENDER
YOURSELVES TO ME AND I WILL TOUCH YOU. I
WILL BLESS YOU; I WILL ALWAYS BE WITH YOU.
YOU WILL NEVER EVER HAVE TO BE AFRAID OF
ANYONE OR ANYTHING BECAUSE I AM WITH YOU.
LOVE ME, BELIEVE IN ME, HAVE FAITH IN ME. YES,
I HAVE CALLED YOU FOR SUCH A TIME AS THIS.
MANY NEED ME BECAUSE SO MANY OF THEIR
FAMILIES HAVE LOST THEIR WAY. MANY ARE
HURTING BECAUSE THEY CAN'T TALK TO THEIR
FAMILY MEMBERS THAT ARE LOST. THEY MUST

PLACE ALL OF THEIR CARES IN MY HAND AND
KNOW AND BELIEVE AND TRUST ME TO TAKE CARE
OF ALL OF THEIR FAMILY, ALL OF THEIR NEEDS.
BUT THEY MUST BE BORN AGAIN AND BELIEVE.
THE FLESH HAS NO PLACE WITH ME. I HATE
FLESH; I HATE THE SMELL OF FLESH. THEY MUST
SURRENDER THEIR ALL IN ORDER FOR ME TO
HELP THEM AND THEIR FAMILY MEMBERS. YIELD
TO ME AND I WILL DO THE REST. READ MY WORD
AS THOUGH THEY ARE EATING THREE MEALS A
DAY. FOLLOW MY WILL, FOLLOW MY WAY, FAST
AND PRAY AND THEIR LIVES WILL BE CHANGED
FOREVER. TAKE THE TIME DAILY AND SPEND
WITH ME. THE SHOOTINGS ARE SATAN ON THE
RAMPAGE. MANY OF THE SHOOTERS DON'T KNOW
WHAT HAS HAPPENED TO THEM. THEIR MINDS
HAVE BEEN OVERTAKEN BY SATAN, THAT'S WHY
WHEN THEY SHOOT, THEY EXPERIENCE AN OUT-
OF-BODY EXPERIENCE, IT'S BECAUSE SATAN HAS
TAKEN OVER. THEY SEE WHAT THEY ARE DOING
BUT THEY CAN'T BELIEVE WHAT THEY ARE DOING.
THEIR FAMILIES ARE EVEN DEVASTATED BECAUSE
THAT'S NOT THE PERSON THEY ALL KNEW. IT'S
BECAUSE SATAN TOOK OVER IN THE MIND OF
THAT PERSON. I CALLED THEM TOO, BUT THEY
COULD NOT HEAR MY VOICE. THEY ENJOYED THE
THINGS OF THE WORLD AND COULD NOT HEAR

ME CALLING THEM, DURING THE NIGHT, DURING
THEIR DREAMS. JUST A WHISPER IN THEIR EARS,
BUT THEY DROWNED ME OUT WITH THE NOISE OF
THE WORLD, THE THINGSOF THE WORLD, AND
SATAN CAPTURED THEM.

PART 2- 10:00 a.m.

CALL UPON ME, CAST YOUR CARES UPON ME,
BELIEVE IN ME, TRUST IN ME, LOVE ME, PUT ME
FIRST. GIVE YOUR LIFE TO ME BY SURRENDERING
TO ME, SURRENDERING TO ME, SURRENDERING TO
ME, LOVING ME MORE THAN YOU LOVE YOURSELF.
NEVER PUT ANY PERSON, PLACE, OR THING
BEFORE ME.

PRAY TO ME; BELIEVE IN ME WITH YOUR HEART
AND NOT YOUR HEAD. IT WILL TAKE TOTAL
SURRENDERING TO ME IN ORDER FOR THE
CHANGE TO COME INTO YOUR LIFE AND INTO
YOUR FAMILY'S LIVES. I LOVE ALL OF YOU, BUT
YOU MUST LOVE ME AND KEEP ME FIRST AND
NOT AN AFTERTHOUGHT WHEN YOUR FAMLY
GETS IN TROUBLE. BELIEVE IN ME DURING THE
GOOD TIMES AND THE BAD TIMES WILL NOT BE
AS BAD BECAUSE YOU WILL HAVE MY STRENGTH
TO ENDURE WHATEVER LIFE BRINGS YOUR WAY.

TRUST ME, BELIEVE ME, LOVE ME, SPEND TIME
WITH ME. FAST, PRAY, TURN FROM YOUR WICKED
WAYS AND HUMBLE YOURSELF TO ME. LOOK UNTO
ME AND KNOW THAT I WILL BE THERE; I WILL
ALWAYS BE THERE WHEN YOU YIELD YOUR HEART,
MIND, AND SOUL TO ME.

I WILL ALWAYS BE IN THE MIDST OF THEE.
BELIEVE ME, TRUST ME, HAVE FAITH IN ME,
NOT WHAT YOU CAN SEE BUT WHAT YOU SIMPLY
BELIEVE WITHIN YOUR HEART, KNOW THAT I
AM WITH YOU. THEY THAT WORSHIP ME, MUST
WORSHIP ME IN SPIRIT AND IN TRUTH.

July 7-5, 2022 8:36 a.m.
A PROPHETIC SONG

"NEVER LET GO"

HOLD MY HAND AND NEVER LET GO. I AM IN YOUR
HEART, I FEEL EVERYTHING YOU FEEL. DON'T
LET GO OF ME FOR I AM WITH YOU, I AM WITH
YOU. NEVER LET GO, NEVER LET GO, NEVER LET
GO. FOR I AM WITH YOU, I AM WITH YOU, I AM
WITH YOU. LOOK UP AND FEEL MY PRESENCE; SEE
ME EVERYWHERE, IN THE TREES, THE FLOWERS,
THE ANIMALS, THE BIRDS, AND THE WIND. I
WILL ALWAYS BE WITH YOU. NEVER LET GO OF

MY HAND. I AM WITH YOU; I AM WITH YOU AND FOR YOU. NEVER LET GO OF ME. HOLD ON; HOLD ON TO ME, HOLD ON TO ME, NEVER LET GO. STAY FOCUSED ON ME AND SEE ME, HEAR ME, NEVER LET GO. LIFT YOUR HANDS TO ME, AND KNOW THAT I AM WITH YOU AND I WILL ALWAYS BE WITH YOU. NEVER LET GO OF ME, FOR I WILL ALWAYS BE WITH YOU.

NEVER LET GO.

July 13, 2022 8:24 p.m.

I didn't give you The Spirit Of FEAR, but the Spirit of Power, Love, and a Sound Mind.

Stay focused on Me and not what Satan is trying to do. Resist him and he will flee. Continue reading My Word to build up your inner Spirit Man. Read Psalm 91, which is My Word for your protection three times per day for one week. My Word will not return void, but you must have faith. Trust and believe in Me and My Word and not in man.

You must stay strong and bold so that I can use you for My glory. Be who I have called you to be. Satan is trying to distract you and stop your destiny that I have already planned for you. Speak to him and <u>command</u> him, <u>The Spirit Of FEAR</u>, to leave your mind and your heart in My Son's name.

Rejoice and Stay in Peace.

Thus Saith the Lord.

July 13, 2022 1:32 p.m.

Yield to the Holy Ghost, Yield to the Holy Ghost today, for tomorrow might be too late. I will forgive and forget your past. Start a new life with Me and have eternal life. There is nothing in the world for you to hang on to. The world will keep you from having eternal life with Me. Time is drawing nigh. Don't let it be too late for you. The door is slowly closing. The dark is getting darker. You must choose the light and the life of eternal life with Me if you want to spend eternal life with your loved ones that are already with Me. They will be waiting for you, but you must yield your heart, mind, and soul to me in order to be with them. Give up your life of sin, give up your life of drugs, give up your life of destruction, and come to Me. I will restore you; I will restore everything you have lost because of what you have done in your past. Yield it all to Me and have eternal life. Remember, I hate the Lust of the Eyes, the Lust of the Flesh, and the Pride of Life. Yield to My will and not your will; yield to My understanding and not your understanding. I know your beginning, the middle, and the end of your life. Yield to Me and have Eternal Life, before the door closes, before the dark gets darker.

Yield to Me, Saith the Lord.

July 22, 2022 9:05 a.m. – 9:13 a.m.

Believe in My Word. Trust My Word; do not be persuaded by the things of the world. Satan is determined to steal, kill, and destroy. Fight with My Word; fast and pray in order to remain strong as a lion and bold as a lion. Satan will use whomever he pleases in order to destroy. He will distract, he will lie, he will deceive, and he will trick. Manipulation is what he loves using in order to capture his prey. Remember, if you love Me, then believe in Me, trust My Word. Give your heart, mind, and soul to Me, and Satan cannot touch you. Stay focused on Me, keep looking up to Me as the Author and Finisher of your faith.

My Word is true and it will not return to Me void. Stay in love and stay in peace. Where My spirit is, there is liberty, freedom, love, peace, joy, happiness, and no fear.

Thus, Saith the Lord.

July 26, 2022 9:09 a.m. -9:24 a.m.

Look unto the hills from which cometh your help; your help comes from Me. I will never leave you nor forsake you. You abide in Me and My Word abides in you. Ask what you will and it shall be in My Son's name, the name of Jesus which is above every name. Every knee shall bow and every tongue will confess that He is Lord.

Judge not or you will be judged. Forgive and forget the past. The past will keep you in the position of being stuck. Move out of Park and go forward in Drive. I have so much for you to do and receive, but you cannot do or receive in Park. Open your heart in order to receive. I will only give you good things and not bad or evil things.

Remember negativism comes from Satan; I will whisper positive words to you and build you up. Satan is the destroyer; understand the difference. I am Love and I love everyone. I have prepared a place for you, but you must knock and the door will open. Enter my gate of Thanksgiving; the more you thank Me and love Me for who I am, the more you will receive. The more you give to others, the more you will receive from Me. The key to your success is loving Me, loving the unlovable, giving to others, keeping Me and My Word first in your life above all others, seeking My Word, and doing My Word. Yield your heart, mind and soul to me.

Thus, Saith the Lord.

July 27, 2022 7:30 a.m. – 7:56 a.m.

Trust my word and lean not unto your own understanding. In all your ways, acknowledge Me. You cannot analyze Me or figure Me out, for I am Spirit and you must know Me in the Spirit.

My ways are not your ways. You must trust Me in everything concerning yourself. I am King of Kings and Lord of Lords and there is no one else above Me. Man will have good intentions, but you can always put your trust in Me because man can fail you and I will not. As you pray in My Word, you can ask what you may and I will perform it, for My Word will never return to Me void but you must have Faith and believe that you received when you pray.

Stand on My Word until you receive the manifestation of

what you asked for. Don't let go of My Word and your Faith.

Thus Saith the Lord.

Chapter 3

SCRIPTURES FOR CRISIS COUNSELING TOPICS

Useful Nuggets as a Crisis and Trauma Counselor
Dr. H. Norman Wright: *The Complete Guide to Crisis & Trauma Counseling*

➢ A crisis is a sudden upsetting event – sometime foreseen, often not – that strikes people in a vulnerable place at a bad time. The English word is based on the Greek term *krinein*, which means "to decide." Crises are life-changing, in part because decisions must be made that nearly always alter the course of life. See additional highlighted notes on handout attached, titled "Crises And Crisis Intervention" by H. Norman Wright

➢ Do not be a lone ranger in counseling – have at least two to three people who you can trust, competent, and mature in Christ that takes the Bible as it is. Choose two to three friends who will be truthful and tell you what is right and what is wrong, not someone that will is always tell you what you want to hear. You will burn out these two to three friends. Jesus had three friends

➢ Learn to listen, not talk. Do not be afraid to just listen. 70% of counseling is listening, 10% is you talking, and 20% is you and the counselee interrupting.

> You need to allow people to grieve to feel the pain, to process; this is all part of the healing.

> The first 30 minutes of a crisis can make or break a situation. What you say during a crisis moment will almost suddenly be forgotten because the person is mentally not there with you listening to what you are saying. The person can be in a state of shock, sometime like a zombie, in a state of disbelief. Sometimes they might ask themselves, why not me? Why did God do this? What could I have done differently? Why didn't I see the signs of trouble with that person?

> Don't be afraid to say "I Don't Know" because as a counselor, you will not know or have the answer to everything, which is why it is important to have a circle of friends you can refer clients to when you have a situation you cannot handle.

> God has never used a perfect person.

Crisis Counseling
Topics with scriptures for use in
counseling sessions
The Holy Bible, English Standard
Version Public Domain

1. Codependency

(Galatians 1:10)

For am I now seeking the
approval of man, or of God?
Or am I trying to please man?
If I were still trying to please
man, I would not be a servant of
Christ.

2. Addiction

(1 Corinthians 10:13)

No temptation has overtaken
you that is not common to man.
God is faithful, and he will not
let you be tempted beyond your
ability, but with the temptation
he will also provide the way of
escape, that you may be able to

endure it.

3. Physical Abuse

(Romans 13:8-10)

Owe no one anything, except to love each other, for the one who loves another has fulfilled the law. For the commandments, "You shall not commit adultery, You shall not murder, You shall not steal, You shall not covet," and any other commandment, are summed up in this word: "You shall love your neighbor as yourself." Love does no wrong to a neighbor; therefore love is the fulfilling of the law.

4. Sexual Abuse

(Leviticus 20:10-16)

"If a man commits adultery with the wife of his neighbor, both the adulterer and the adulteress shall surely be put to death. If a man lies with his father's wife, he has uncovered his father's nakedness; both of them shall surely be put to death; their blood is upon them. If a man lies with his daughter-in-law, both of them shall surely be put to death; they have committed perversion; their blood is upon them. If a man lies with a male as with a woman, both of them have committed an abomination; they shall surely be put to death; their blood is upon them. If a man takes a woman and her mother also, it is depravity; he and they shall be burned with fire, that there may be no depravity among you. ...

5. Anger

(Psalm 37:8)

Refrain from anger, and forsake

wrath! Fret not yourself; it
tends only to evil.

6. Eating Disorders

(1 Corinthians 6:19-20)

Or do you not know that your
body is a temple of the Holy
Spirit within you, whom you
have from God? You are not
your own, for you were bought
with a price. So glorify God in
your body.

7. Death

(Romans 14:8)

For if we live, we live to the
Lord, and if we die, we die to
the Lord. So then, whether we
live or whether we die, we are
the Lord's.

8. *Divorce Recovery*

(1 Corinthians 7:15)

But if the unbelieving partner separates, let it be so. In such cases the brother or sister is not enslaved. God has called you to peace.

9. *Remarriage*

(1 Corinthians 7:39)

A wife is bound to her husband as long as he lives. But if her husband dies, she is free to be married to whom she wishes, only in the Lord

10. *Dying*

(John 14:1-3)

"Let not your hearts be troubled. Believe in God; believe also in me. In my Father's house are many rooms. If it were not so, would I have told you that I go to prepare a place for you? And if I go and

prepare a place for you, I will
come again and will take you
to myself, that where I am you
may be also.

11. *Faith*

(Ephesians 2:8)

For by grace you have been
saved through faith. And this is
not your own doing; it is the gift
of God,

12. *Discipline Of Children*

(Proverbs 13:24)

Whoever spares the rod hates
his son, but he who loves him is
diligent to discipline him.

13. *Low Self Esteem*

(Philippians 4:13)

I can do all things through him
who strengthens me

14. Forgiveness

(Mark 11:25)

And whenever you stand praying, forgive, if you have anything against anyone, so that your Father also who is in heaven may forgive you your trespasses.

15. Repentance

(Acts 2:38)

And Peter said to them, "Repent and be baptized every one of you in the name of Jesus Christ for the forgiveness of your sins, and you will receive the gift of the Holy Spirit.

16. Spiritual Brokenness

(Psalm 51:17)

The sacrifices of God are a broken spirit; a broken and contrite heart, O God, you will not despise.

17. Boundaries

(2 Corinthians 6:14)

Do not be unequally yoked
with unbelievers. For what
partnership has righteousness
with lawlessness? Or what
fellowship has light with
darkness?

18. Communication In Marriage

(1 Peter 3:1-9)

Likewise, wives, be subject to
your own husbands, so that
even if some do not obey the
word, they may be won without
a word by the conduct of their
wives, when they see your
respectful and pure conduct.
Do not let your adorning be
external—the braiding of hair
and the putting on of gold
jewelry, or the clothing you
wear— but let your adorning
be the hidden person of the
heart with the imperishable

beauty of a gentle and quiet
spirit, which in God's sight is
very precious. For this is how
the holy women who hoped in
God used to adorn themselves,
by submitting to their own
husbands.

19. Premarital Relations

(Hebrews 13:4)

Let marriage be held in honor
among all, and let the marriage
bed be undefiled, for God will
judge the sexually immoral and
adulterous.

20. Christian Husbands

(1 Peter 3:7)

Likewise, husbands, live with
your wives in an understanding
way, showing honor to the
woman as the weaker vessel,
since they are heirs with you
of the grace of life, so that your
prayers may not be hindered.

21. *Christian Wives*

(1 Peter 3:1-22)

Likewise, wives, be subject to
your own husbands, so that
even if some do not obey the
word, they may be won without
a word by the conduct of their
wives, when they see your
respectful and pure conduct.
Do not let your adorning be
external—the braiding of hair
and the putting on of gold
jewelry, or the clothing you
wear— but let your adorning
be the hidden person of the
heart with the imperishable
beauty of a gentle and quiet
spirit, which in God's sight is
very precious. For this is how
the holy women who hoped in
God used to adorn themselves,
by submitting to their own
husbands.

22. *Inner Healing*

(Psalm 73:26)

My flesh and my heart may fail,
but God is the strength of my
heart and my portion forever.

23. *Spiritual Abuse*

(<u>Ephesians 6:12</u>)

For we do not wrestle against
flesh and blood, but against the
rulers, against the authorities,
against the cosmic powers over
this present darkness, against
the spiritual forces of evil in the
heavenly places.

24. *Anxiety And Depression*

(<u>1 Corinthians 10:13</u>)

No temptation has overtaken
you that is not common to man.
God is faithful, and he will not
let you be tempted beyond your
ability, but with the temptation
he will also provide the way of
escape, that you may be able to
endure it

25. *Anxious*

(Philippians 4:6-7)

Do not be anxious about anything, but in everything by prayer and supplication with thanksgiving let your requests be made known to God. And the peace of God, which surpasses all understanding, will guard your hearts and your minds in Christ Jesus.

Chapter 4

LIFE EMERGENCY SCRIPTURES

King James Version
Public domain

(Psalm 46:1KJV) - God *is* our refuge and strength, a very present help in trouble.

(Psalm 68:6 KJV) - God setteth the solitary in families: he bringeth out those which are bound with chains: but the rebellious dwell in a dry *land*.

(Proverbs 3:5-6 KJV) - Trust in the LORD with all thine heart; and lean not unto thine own understanding. In all thy ways acknowledge him, and he shall direct thy paths.

(Matthew 7:7 KJV) - Ask, and it shall be given you; seek, and ye shall find; knock, and it shall be opened unto you.

(Hebrews 4:15-16 KJV) - For we have not an high priest which cannot be touched with the feeling of our infirmities; but was in all points tempted like as *we are, yet* without sin. Let us therefore come boldly unto the throne of grace, that we may obtain mercy, and find grace to help in time of need.

(1 Chronicles 4:10 KJV) - And Jabez called on the God of Israel, saying, Oh that thou wouldest bless me indeed, and enlarge my coast, and that thine hand might be with me,

and that thou wouldest keep *me* from evil, that it may not grieve me! And God granted him that which he requested.

(2 Chronicles 14:11 KJV) - And Asa cried unto the LORD his God, and said, LORD, *it is* nothing with thee to help, whether with many, or with them that have no power: help us, O LORD our God; for we rest on thee, and in thy name, we go against this multitude. O LORD, thou *art* our God; let not man prevail against thee.

(Psalm 10:14 KJV) - Thou hast seen *it*; for thou beholdest mischief and spite, to requite *it* with thy hand: the poor committeth himself unto thee; thou art the helper of the fatherless.

(Psalm 27:9 KJV) - Hide not thy face *far* from me; put not thy servant away in anger: thou hast been my help; leave me not, neither forsake me, O God of my salvation.
(Psalm 37:40 KJV) - And the LORD shall help them, and deliver them: he shall deliver them from the wicked, and save them, because they trust in him.

(Psalm 40:17 KJV) - But I *am* poor and needy; *yet* the Lord thinketh upon me: thou *art* my help and my deliverer; make no tarrying, O my God.

(Psalm 60:11 KJV) - Give us help from trouble: for

vain *is* the help of man.

(Psalm 63:7 KJV) - Because thou hast been my help, therefore in the shadow of thy wings will I rejoice.

(Psalm 146:5 KJV) - Happy *is he* that *hath* the God of Jacob for his help, whose hope *is* in the LORD his God.

(Isaiah 41:10 KJV) - Do not fear, for I am with you; do not be afraid, for I am your God. I will strengthen you; I will surely help you; I will uphold you with My right hand of righteousness.

(Isaiah 41:13 KJV) - For I the LORD thy God will hold thy right hand, saying unto thee, Fear not; I will help thee.

(Mark 9:24 KJV) - And straightway the father of the child cried out, and said with tears, Lord, I believe; help thou mine unbelief.

(John 14:26 KJV) - But the Comforter, *which is* the Holy Ghost, whom the Father will send in my name, he shall teach you all things, and bring all things to your remembrance, whatsoever I have said unto you.

Chapter 5

FINAL PROPHETIC SCRIBES TO ENCOURAGE DURING THE WORLD OF CHAOS 2022

August 6, 2022 3:20 p.m. - 3:38 p.m.

A Word from the Lord received while sitting on the porch while raining outside

Listen to the rain. As it rains, so I shower you down with My blessings, blessings from the North, South, East, and West. See My Glory as it pours, as it rains. There will be no lack in your life, no lack for whatever you want. Hear My rain, as it's soothing to your spirit, soothing to your heart, soothing to your mind. Listen to the thunder as I command the earth to be still and know that I am God. I am God of all things, in the beginning and in the end.

Man cannot tame the rain, man cannot stop the rain, man cannot stop the thunder; it all happens by My command. See and hear My glory, see and hear My glory. Feel My glory with the wind that you cannot see. My wind is like Faith, you cannot see but you must believe. The wind is My Breath, breathing upon you. Enjoy My touch, for it is My healing touch; the touch that will heal your mind, your soul, your heart, your body.

Breathe in, breathe out. I have control over your breathing. As easy as you breathe, life can stop or life can continue. Breathe. By My command will be whether you live or die. I chose you today to breathe the breath of life and not die today. Worship Me, glorify Me, and live a good life living for Me. The trees move when I say move; they bow down to Me, as I command them to. They live only by My command. When their season is over, they too must die. I am that I am, there is none other; no other God but Me.

Enjoy My breath of life as the winds continue blowing upon you. Enjoy My healing touch, the touch of Me, the touch of heavenly life from above. Breathe Life.

Thus, Saith the Lord.

August 25, 2022 10:29 a.m. -10:35 a.m.

Wait On the Lord.

Wait on Me, for I will renew your strength. My Word that I gave to you will not return void to Me. Stay focused, stay strong. Don't look to the left or to the right, for surely what you asked for will surely come.

Wait, wait, wait. My ways are not your ways, My timing is not your timing. Read My Word and stay in peace. As you stay in peace, what you asked for will surely come.
Worrying will stop your Faith in Me and My Word and what you asked for will be delayed. Remember, Satan does

not want you to have what you desire to have; it is My will but you must believe. Have Faith, trust, and believe within your heart, not your head. Just thank Me for giving you what you have asked for; this will cause the manifestation from the spiritual realm to the physical realm.

Wait, wait, wait.

Thus, Saith The Lord.

September 1, 2022 10:28 a.m. – 10:46 a.m.

Stay focused on Me no matter what's happening around you in the world. I will continue to keep you in peace as you focus only on Me. Satan tries to distract and destroy you mentally, physically, and spiritually with his antics. Pay him no attention. Laugh at his attempts because he is a loser. He can never win, but he keeps trying. He pulls out everything he can to win, but he will indeed fail. Pay him no attention as you continue reading my word, fasting and praying, enjoying life even if it seems like things are falling apart around you.

Believe with your heart that I am the Almighty God; I am the Prince of Peace. Keep looking up to the heavens and feel My peace, My love, My joy. Not as man gives it, but as I give it to you. My peace, love, and joy are eternal, but man's peace, love, and joy are temporary.

Trust Me, love Me., keep me in your heart and in your thoughts, and you will have peace. Keep My Word before your eyes and you will remain in peace. Give no thought to the negative things that are happening, for they will surely change, but not until the world bow down and worship Me and not want the things of the world more than they want Me.

Put nothing and no one before Me. My son went to the Cross for such a time as this. Did they forget that He went to the Cross? Surely, they have forgotten. Did their forefathers put their Trust in me? Surely, they have forgotten. They must repent, turn from their wicked ways, seek my face; and only then will I heal their land.

Thus, Saith the Lord.

My arms are folded until they repent from their heart and not their head. Repent means to Turn, turn, turnaround from what you are doing.

Thus, Saith the Lord.
Lift your hands unto me and repent.

Thus, Saith the Lord.

Chapter 6

CONCLUSION

In conclusion, I have shared with you a portion of my God-inspired personal spiritual journal. God inspired Prophetic Scribes to share with others that God would allow me to share in this book.

Due to the tremendous amount of turmoil that people are experiencing during these times in our lives, I felt compelled to share some of my nuggets and specific topical scriptures from my crisis and trauma classes that I completed at Laurel University. I have also shared with you scriptures that at a quick glance may assist you when dealing with your personal emergency situations.

A Prayer of Salvation

"Dear God, I know I'm a sinner, and I ask for your forgiveness. I believe Jesus Christ is Your Son. I believe that He died for my sin and that you raised Him to life. I want to trust Him as my Savior and follow Him as Lord, from this day forward. Guide my life and help me to do your will. I pray this in the name of Jesus. Amen."

I pray that God will bless you in finding your Destiny as to who He is to you and who you are to Him...who did He create you to be?

Sariba